# Southern Coastal Living

## STYLISH LOWCOUNTRY HOMES BY J BANKS DESIGN

# Southern Coastal Living

## STYLISH LOWCOUNTRY HOMES BY J BANKS DESIGN

**JONI VANDERSLICE**

WITH JUDITH NASATIR

PHOTOGRAPHS BY ANDREW & GEMMA INGALLS

**GIBBS SMITH**
TO ENRICH AND INSPIRE HUMANKIND

20 19 18 17 16          5 4 3 2 1

Published by
Gibbs Smith
P.O. Box 667
Layton, Utah 84041
1.800.835.4993 orders
www.gibbs-smith.com

Developed in collaboration with: Jill Cohen Associates, LLC

Design template by Rita Sowins
Printed and bound in Hong Kong

Gibbs Smith books are printed on either recycled, 100% post-consumer waste,
FSC-certified papers or on paper produced from sustainable PEFC-certified forest/
controlled wood source. Learn more at www.pefc.org.

Library of Congress Cataloging-in-Publication Data

Names: Vanderslice, Joni, author.
Title: Southern coastal living : stylish Lowcountry homes by J Banks Design /
Joni Vanderslice with Judith Nasatir.
Description: First Edition. | Layton, Utah : Gibbs Smith, 2016.
Identifiers: LCCN 2016008057 | ISBN 9781423644415 (hardcover)
Subjects: LCSH: Interior decoration--South Atlantic States. | J Banks Design.
Classification: LCC NK2004.3.J3 V36 2016 | DDC 747.0975--dc23
LC record available at http://lccn.loc.gov/2016008057

TO RICK, SARAH, AND GRACE—
GOD HAS GIVEN US A LIFE FULL OF ADVENTURE!
I LOVE AND THRIVE ON YOUR PASSION FOR PEOPLE
AND FOR SHARING ALL THINGS GOOD.

# Contents

# Introduction

Every person who has a story to tell wants to share it. Perhaps that is, at least in part, the seed of the idea of southern hospitality. Hospitality is about making people who arrive somewhere other than home feel at home: that they're in capable hands, they can relax, their needs will be met, they can be themselves as they want to be whether they are inside or in nature. That is a deep emotional connection. It is what I call a sense of place. It is what design, at its best, when it's right, creates.

In the South, we have a tradition of wanting our interiors to express who we are—and where we are. In our primary residences, we tend to show our life histories. For our second homes, we may often craft a different personality. Because we're southern, and because collecting seems to be a part of the DNA of the South, we do much of this through the accumulation of objects, artwork, and countless photographs of family and friends.

Good taste is not an abstract ideal for me, but a tangible concept personal to each client. I want to capture each of my clients' personal vision with the same passion as if it were my own. To do so, I ask my clients how they live; how they utilize space; if they like to entertain; to show me images of what they like; and even more telling, images of what they don't like. After I have a true sense of the client's lifestyle, I can bring in color palettes that reflect their natural preferences, texture and furnishings that reflect their personalities, and unique art or accessories that are personal to them.

I love that the houses my designers and I work in today are made for the way we live today; yet they almost always carry forward traces, though very faint ones, of the traditions and vernaculars of our historic regional building and decorating styles. On Hilton Head Island, where southern coastal style is dominant, we use relaxed rather than formal references to signal the design heritage of the wider region. To express the spirit of an old house in a newly built one, we might use shifting rooflines and different building materials to suggest that additions were made to the main house over the years. If we use columns inside a home as opposed to outside, they will have simple forms and understated capitals with little ornament. There will be a proper entry, gracious porches and verandas for catching the breeze, a back hall mudroom for practicality, shutters and panels, shades and screens, and so on.

*I am a great believer in the role that interior design plays in creating a home that exudes hospitality. For me, this means an aesthetic of luxury without pretense—the comfortable sophistication that is the essence of southern coastal style.*

All of these features belong to the tradition of the southern house. Today we use them still, but in the casual forms that suit life as we live it here and now. If a house is meant to be unpretentious and cottage-like in feeling, as so many houses in coastal resort areas such as Hilton Head are, shake and board and batten serve the purpose—and feel quintessentially coastal.

think I have always known that there was power in design and interiors. I grew up in High Point, North Carolina, the capital of America's furniture industry. As early as 4th grade, I remember saying I wanted to be an interior designer. Throughout my childhood, I was always trying to do something to my room and to the house. All my extracurricular projects were about designing rooms and furniture. I don't know where my love of interior design came from, because no one in my family was interested or involved in it. My father was entrepreneur in auto racing and airplanes and heavy equipment. My mother was an accountant. But I never wavered through high school, and I received my bachelor's degree in interior design from East Carolina University.

Putting down roots on Hilton Head was never the plan. I came here with a group of girls just after graduation to spend the summer. Very quickly, through a friend of a friend, I met Charles Fraser, the pioneering developer and a mastermind of the use of protective deeds and covenants, who planned Hilton Head and so many other ecologically friendly southern coastal communities, and his wife, Mary. When Mary found out that I had an interior design degree, she asked if I would come work with them, as they were renovating the Sea Pines properties then and she needed someone to liaise with the designers and also to collaborate with her on those she was redoing herself and, if all went well, perhaps do some of them myself.

Working for the Frasers that summer was a tremendous experience. In retrospect, it had a profound impact on my life. Charles would pull me up into his office for planning meetings for other developments, which gave me an incredible opportunity to learn about building firsthand. One of my jobs was to organize their photo library. They traveled frequently and had amassed a really rich archive of design-related images—bicycle stands, lampposts, bridges, gates, you name it—from their trips all over Europe and elsewhere. The daily effect of living on Hilton Head, which he developed so brilliantly while preserving both the landscape and the wildlife, influenced my own passion for the environment. It certainly gave me the impetus years later for building the Lowcountry's first LEED-certified building, which houses my firm.

Toward the end of that first summer on Hilton Head, Mary, who thought I dressed well, asked if I would put together a wardrobe for their elder daughter, who was off to boarding school. I did, and she loved it. So did Mary, who then asked me to do the same for their other daughter, and then for herself. Through Mary's recommendation,

I ended up with a clientele and so took a career detour into the fashion industry.

In those days, Savannah had a wonderful family-owned department store called Fines. Mr. Fine had the area's most up-to-date sportswear department, so I would shop there and bring the clothes back to Hilton Head for my clients. Eventually, he asked me to work for him, promising to take me under his wing and teach me to buy in New York. He did. At that time, especially in the South, most women and young women built their wardrobes on dresses or country separates from Pendleton and the like. But the industry was rapidly shifting to separates—sportswear—and Mr. Fine needed someone who knew how to put separates together for his in-store fashion shows, store windows, and young women's department. I was just a year out of college, and it was an incredible opportunity. The job at Fines led to another job at a very high-end clothing store on Hilton Head that was launching a new women's and children's boutique; that job led to one at another high-end clothing store, as buyer and manager. I knew, though, that fashion wasn't where I wanted my career to be. Not long after, I was offered a position in an interior design firm, where I soon became its design manager.

O n Hilton Head in those days, if people wanted great residential interiors, they brought in designers from elsewhere. My initial goal was to change that. When the firm was invited to do a show house—my very first one—it was a chance to make it clear that we on Hilton Head were capable of more than the so-called "resort look"—the flowered sofas, the rattan, the sea foam green and mauve color palettes—that was so prevalent then. My house didn't look like that, nor did most of the rest of the world's. Traditional, always a favorite look in the South, was definitely "in" in those days, thanks to Parish-Hadley, Mark Hampton, Mario Buatta, and others. For the show house, I went traditional but with a twist: I created a deep green bedroom aflame with a camellia-red print. It was inspired by Mario Buatta, but I mixed in many more linens and seaside references, a meld of two of my favorite looks. That, for me, was really the beginning.

Soon after, some developer clients commissioned me to design the reception center for the Melrose Club, an innovative resort community they had planned to build on Daufuskie Island, a barrier island just off the coast of Hilton Head and reachable only by boat. Their overall vision included a 52-room inn in the style of an old plantation house, 50 four-bedroom cottages, an equestrian center, and a Jack Nicklaus–designed golf course. The reception center, with a decorative scheme that was full-on coastal traditional, antiques included, was phase one. Next was the equestrian center, which we also did. As for the remaining interiors, my clients had made it clear from the outset that they intended to hire a hospitality design specialist. When they couldn't find one that understood the essence of Lowcountry Daufuskie Island living, they commissioned me to make a presentation.

Even at its most sophisticated, southern coastal style has a relaxed, easy feel that suits the indoor/ outdoor lifestyle. Lighter, brighter interiors contain more color and less clutter. Stylish, comfortable furnishings are key, as are fabrics and finishes that wear beautifully.

That project launched me in the resort and golf club business, and it snowballed very quickly. The owner of the design firm then sold me the business, which I was able to purchase with the help of my developer clients, who wanted a design firm that would be able to focus on their resort properties. I was all of 28 at the time, and there were some major hiccups in the early years. Having grown up in a family business, though, I have always been comfortable in business mode. My father always talked to me about business. From the time I was small, he would take me with him everywhere; while he was working, I would sit in a corner with a book. Even after I moved to Hilton Head, he would talk through deals with me. It was such a wonderful upbringing, and most unusual in its way for a girl.

When I took over the design firm, we had 12 designers on staff, many of them without a formal design education. My vision for the future of the business focused on having a staff of professionals, all graduates of accredited, four-year design programs. At the time, this was a radical idea for a design firm in a resort area. Yet over the past three decades, we've become that and more. Today, we are an award-winning 45-person firm, internationally renowned for both residential and hospitality projects. One of my designers has shared the entire journey; another has been with me almost as long; a large cadre has been with J Banks for more than 15 years.

We are distinctive in that we do both residential and hospitality interiors, often very large ones, many of them overseas, from Mexico to Italy and beyond. In part, our twin focus has come about naturally because our residential clients go to our resorts and belong to our clubs, and vice-versa. Both types of projects develop from the same design principles and thought process: first and foremost, insight into the client's needs and lifestyle; a feel for site, cultural context, and geography; planning; and attention to detail. What differentiates the two types of projects is scale. What connects the two is that we understand resort and hospitality, at home and away from home. Here on Hilton Head, we live it, breathe it, and design for it every single day. One of the many things that people learn when they move to the southern coastal region is that formal does not mean here what it does, or once did, elsewhere. There is such a thing as luxury without pretense. It starts with comfort and hospitality. When we are comfortable in our home and it expresses the essence of who we are in a relaxed way, others become comfortable in it from the moment they walk through the door. This is the heart of our southern coastal lifestyle. Here, luxury does not mean crystal chandeliers, dark paneling, and elaborate drapes. It is not a quality found only in the interior. Luxury can be outside. Casual can be formal. A dinner on the lawn at a table set with candles and silver, crystal, and bone china can be the most luxurious dinner ever.

*The relationship between the senses of sight and touch is fascinating. Intriguing contrasts between refined and more rustic finishes always enhance our visual and tactile experience.*

T hinking about how people actually interact with a space—and how we want them to—is the foundation of everything that my designers and I do. Life on the southern coast is an indoor/outdoor life for most of the year. Determining how best to use outdoor spaces is critical, as are the elements of design that connect the interior with the exterior.

The coastal sense of place begins with the view, because that water view—and the landscape itself—is defining. It draws people to it, and into it, which is why people vacation, live, and have second homes along the coast. That, in turn, is why we layer a home's living and entertaining spaces into the landscape with deep porches and patios furnished like living and dining rooms, a grill area, pool, pool house, outdoor kitchen, fireplace, and fire pit, and lawns and gardens of one sort or another. Even a dock becomes an outdoor living and entertaining space, especially in the summer, when it's the one place that reliably catches a breeze.

Coastal living tends to be more relaxed, even at its most classically formal. More people tend to gather day to day in second homes, so we make sure we plan for how to seat everyone, and sleep everyone, and feed everyone. We also make sure that our clients have a well-furnished retreat—often the master bedroom, or an office off the bedroom and away from the main living areas—for privacy when the house is full. In the South and on its shores, and especially in a second home, we tend to want interiors that are lighter and brighter, with more color and less clutter. Fabrics need to be able to stand up to the daily wear of wet bathing suits and sandy feet, of children, their friends, and pets, so performance fabrics come in very handy. Furnishings, especially seating, should be comfortable for lounging, for flopping, and for those naps that you can only take when you're on holiday. On a winter's evening, the dining table becomes the focal point, so it's important that the chairs encourage people to sit around talking and telling stories until the last flicker of the candle flame.

Analyzing how people use a space and how you want them to use it—that is the essence of what I consider the editing process. Editing is everything in design, and we work very hard to get it right, meaning that we make sure the essentials are correct and in place. Interestingly, step one of editing, for me, is always about establishing psychological comfort: first I determine the room's focal points—the primary one is almost always the view—and then I figure out what visual cues to give in order to orchestrate how people will experience the space, and then I balance all the elements to create the kind of harmony that is felt and that allows us to relax.

In this part of the country, we must constantly balance light spaces against dark spaces. In the Northeast or the Midwest, the winters are so gray that it's hard to think about battling light. Here, that is what we do daily. Deeper porches, side panels on the windows, and drop-down and/or electronic window shades are smart solutions to this issue. What can be challenging is to persuade light-deprived people who don't live in the region all year around just how blinding the sun will be at 5 o'clock on a summer day. Shutters and louvers, which modulate light beautifully, and curtains, which in this part of the country are more than just window dressing, all serve a similar purpose. They are traditional here, as they are in other coastal regions and sunny climates. And because strong light prefers strong color, the palettes here tend to be more saturated.

In the South, as elsewhere, people come together around food. It is the core of family life and such a deep reflection of who we are. And it is why the kitchen has become a multifunction room that is the heart of the house. So many people seem afraid of entertaining. They needn't be. All that is really necessary to live life with an open door is preparation—a well-stocked fridge and pantry, plus a variety of fun and beautiful things for setting the table—and creativity. I learned this early on from my grandmother. She was a fabulous cook and would pull me into her kitchen whenever I wanted to learn. My grandparents had a farm, along with other ventures, so my grandmother cooked lunch each day for my grandfather. The whole family would often come in for the midday meal, especially during the summer. But my grandmother made it clear that we could stop in anytime. When we did, we knew that there would always be enough. Gathering around her table as part of growing up influenced me more than I can say. I still have her original cookbook, as well as my great-grandmother's. I use them to this day.

still remember preparing my first Thanksgiving dinner at my father's house, where I lived after my parents divorced and my mother remarried. It was also the first time that my grandmother had not made the Thanksgiving dinner. She came a little early to make sure I was all right, critiqued everything, and told me what I had done well. I was so proud. I try to share that kind of experience with my own daughters, Sarah and Grace, as I have found each day of my life made richer though a lifetime of seeing the importance in that.

I now have my grandmother's house in High Point. My whole team stays there when we go twice a year for the furniture market. My husband, Rick, and I and our girls use it when we visit my family there. The core of the house is a little '50s bungalow, to which we've added an outdoor kitchen and entertaining area, among other enhancements. But I've left my grandmother's kitchen just as it was when I was growing up, with a boomerang countertop detailed with chrome and rubber. This house is still where we gather with family, because to us, it is just tradition.

I love that with the tools and skills of our profession, my designers and I are able to make our clients' families and friends—and our own—feel wanted and cared for when they cross the threshold into a home we have created. The greatest lesson that I have learned is that perfection is not what matters. What does matter is the sense of personality and place: that the homes we create make people feel welcome, wanted, relaxed, and happy to share. Those are what I call the comforts of home. Though each of us may express them in our own distinctive fashion, and while they may look and feel different depending on where we live, they are universal.

# My Design Philosophy

nterior design can accomplish many things, but one of its most important roles is to create comfort. I think people naturally relax in a space when they can see clearly how they are meant to use it. Such well-planned, well-organized spaces have great appeal because the designer has not only analyzed every aspect of the room's function but also envisioned precisely how the clients will live in it every day. Inviting architecture sets the stage for all the elements of interior design—palette, furnishings, materials, and so on. But for me, an understanding of how people will live in their home drives all of my design decisions.

Design is a layered process. My initial determination always involves sight lines. In every room, I decide where I want the eye to go first. This is what I call the primary focal point, and every subsequent choice I make follows from it. In the majority of our coastal-style homes, of course, the view is the focus, so that is what I want people to take in and respond to first. Once the primary focus is set, I then develop additional, secondary focal points and use proportion, scale, and color to direct the eye to them organically.

People who live with compelling vistas anywhere know that gorgeous views are wondrous to behold—but not all the time. Even in rooms where the exterior dominates, we need opportunities to turn our backs away from it, to direct our gaze and attention inward. We also need enclosed spaces, which create a specific, intimate kind of coziness; so I advocate and design for them even in our mostly open plans.

Planning how people will use each space is essential. I want people to be able to see themselves in these spaces as we develop them: in that wing chair reading a book by that fireplace; on this porch having a glass of wine at the end of the day, gathered at that table with their family and friends. When people are able to visualize themselves living within a home, they will want to be there—and welcome others there, too. That is where hospitality begins.

Human scale—how the human body relates proportionally to what surrounds it—is critical to my idea of comfort and to how I choose furnishings. I constantly think about and envision how particular clients will interact with the size and proportions of their rooms and their furnishings, with the arrangement of the furnishings in the rooms, and even with the pathways through the home. When I designed my first line of furniture, I rethought everything I knew about scale and proportion. In those days, our primary objective was to create tall furniture to suit spaces with higher ceilings, and lower pieces for smaller rooms. Today, we regularly deal with rooms that have grand proportions, and

*In my point of view, to create comfort a designer must have a good understanding of human scale—that is, how our bodies relate proportionally to the size of the furnishings and the volumes that surround us.*

many of our clients' homes have two-story entry halls and/or great rooms. Yes, we need oversized pieces that fill those spaces suitably. Yet we also want a mix of heights and sizes—of low, mid, and high backs; of single seats, two-seat sofas, and sectionals—where they make sense and for visual interest. Sometimes I like to play with scale—juxtaposing the high with the low, the grand with the not so—just because it is unexpected.

After planning the spatial organization and furniture groupings for function, and then determining the actual scale and type of furniture for the rooms, I move onto the color palette, developing a general color scheme and finishes that will capture a sense of place and personality. Where it feels right, I love to use color to connect the indoors with the outdoors. Where I want a more embracing, cozy feeling, I will adapt the palette accordingly. Next, I start to look at rugs and the decorative lighting that attaches to the ceiling or walls. Then I select lamps and artwork, both of which can make or break a room. Then, and only then, come the accessories.

*From spatial organization and furniture plans to fabric selection and the final details of art and accessories, every design decision I make stems from an understanding of how each client lives—and wishes to live—in their home.*

# Our House

When Rick and I designed this house with our architect, we knew clearly what we wanted: a house that appeared to have evolved over time rather than one that was obviously new construction. The impetus for this came partly from our own preferences and partly from the desire for a house that would embody a sense of history and place while lying lightly and naturally on our waterfront property. In the South, older houses tended to grow over the generations. The owners would build the main portion first, and then the family would slowly add to the original section as necessary through the years. In order to create something contemporary that would resemble this idea in spirit, we decided to vary the rooflines of the different sections. And because we also wanted our home to feel more casual and cottage-like than formal, we opted to use shake and board and batten, which are quintessentially coastal.

Our house is essentially one room deep, with areas that flow organically into one another; all of them, including our master suite at one far end, open to outdoor spaces and the landscape beyond. This type of layout makes so much sense for how we live. It also celebrates the reason we chose this property in the first place: open access to the waterfront and the indoor/outdoor lifestyle that goes with it. Yet there is a potential drawback to the open plan's convenience: big spaces can become too big. As we were working out the interior architecture, we kept devising design features, such as interior columns, to bring each area to human scale. Human scale, I believe, is the starting point of everything when it comes to our physical comfort at home. It is what determines how much open space the eye can take in and yet still exude the coziness that domestic rooms should have.

From our front door, we look straight through the interior to the water. We designed the rear façade of the house to be entirely windows, with French doors that open directly to the furnished verandas and the landscape. The natural secondary focus is our living room, the area to the left of the front door as you enter. A fireplace com-

*Rick and I decided to use a combination of shake and board-and-batten siding as the building materials for this house because they are quintessentially coastal in spirit and give the exterior the casual feel we wanted it to have. From our front door, we look straight through the interior to the water.*

mands attention at one end, while several seating areas organize the overall volume. We have filled them with beloved furnishings and the objects and artwork that we have brought back from our family and professional travels over the years.

Opposite the living area, and to the right of the front door, is our more formal dining area. Banquettes and upholstered chairs encourage our guests to gather at the table and to stay seated long after the meal, telling stories and enjoying the pleasures of each other's company.

In the South, where inclement weather wasn't a problem, historically kitchens were separate from the main house because of the danger of fire. As a result, in older houses the kitchens often appear to have been later attachments to the main house. I wanted to suggest something similar in the design of our kitchen, with white wall cabinets that look as if they had always been there, and ovens and an island that appear to be later additions. Concrete floors in all the ground-level spaces are easy to maintain, and they essentially disappear under the rugs.

The family room (beginning on page 40) is the center of where our everyday life happens, and I wanted it to wrap its arms around us. There are, therefore, fewer windows and a bigger fireplace than in the living room. I had the walls painted a rich, deep ochre, a color inspired by a project I did in Italy, Castello di Casole. The darker, cushier furnishings are very inviting. Big ottomans and lots of pillows supplement the sofas and work wonderfully for when we all watch a movie together or the girls gather here with their friends.

Upstairs are Sarah and Grace's bedrooms, their project room, Rick's study, and my home office. The whole complex feels like a converted attic space. In all of these rooms, the floors are of reclaimed wood. My grandfather, who had collected it from old buildings, had kept it in a barn that is now on my property in High Point. It was interesting to teach the men who laid these floors not to sand the boards down and make them perfect. I love the way they show their age and the original paint that remains on many of them.

*When we walk in the door, the first thing we see is the view; it is our primary focal point. To subtly reinforce*
*that visual emphasis, I placed the long antique table, which I had purchased in England, and the antique patterned*
*runner to direct the eye to the exterior.*

*Facing: My living room includes pieces in various styles and periods. Above: A child's spool chair that I found on a trip to Ireland inspired the larger version that I designed for my furniture line, the J Banks Collection by Stanford Furniture, and covered in one of the Africa-inspired fabrics from my Tanzania Collection by Kravet.*

*Above: Blue-and-white china and tartanware are two of my longstanding loves and part of my southern heritage. I designed this wall unit for grouping some of my favorite pieces for a greater visual impact. Facing: Interior columns and ceiling beams set in different directions create definition between the living and dining areas. Beside the sofa is the antique Irish child's chair that sparked the design for my larger contemporary version.*

# ARTWORK AND COLLECTIONS

Paintings, photographs, and objects—our art and accessories—are the final touches of any home. I believe that all these pieces should have meaning to the homeowner rather than including them just because the colors are right. When these pieces express where we come from, where we've been, how we think and what we enjoy, they tell our story. Some may be serious and significant works, while others are likely to be more casual and informal—those mementoes and items of whimsy that we love because they make us smile. I like to pair them together, often side by side, or show them as a curated collection. This not only creates visual interest and gives the eye relief but also helps to tell a personal tale.

In my home, all the art and the objects have meaning. My collections of blue-and-white porcelain and tartanware are a part of who I am, where I come from, and where I have traveled. My Herend figurines speak directly to my love of animals. I find them charming and delicate, and I always display them as a group for greater impact. I occasionally select several to include as part of the table décor for dinner parties because they invariably make my

guests smile, and me as well. My trove of antique children's chairs, gathered on buying trips abroad, gives me great delight: they remind me of my daughters' childhoods, are uniquely beautiful in themselves, and still function as intended, which my godchildren and my nieces' children have proved happily over the years. Then there are the wonderful Kente cloths and other objects found on our visits to Africa.

There is one painting in particular, by Texas-based artist Donna Howell-Sickles, which I feel illustrates my point perfectly. When I first saw Donna's work at a gallery in Aspen, it just made me happy. As I looked harder at her pieces, I realized that she was the first artist I had seen who painted women not as pretty objects to be admired, but smiling and in control of something. Her central figure, always a woman, might have a bull by the horns, for example. In ours, she holds the reins of a horse. And she wears cowboy boots. There is a dog that represents her guardian angel; a red moon, which indicates fertility; and a river. In other words, the painting is full of symbolism that feels deeply personal to me. The way my woman

*Our own house is full of mementoes, whimsical objects, and more serious and significant artworks. Each piece has its own special meaning and a memory attached to its discovery. Together, they tell our family history.*

holds the reins is very much in my mind how my father saw me. He always told me that I could do anything I wanted to do, and that I could run any business. "Just grow, grab it and go," he would say. He rode horses and wore cowboy boots for every occasion. And, of course, we love dogs, and we live on the water. So I fell in love with Donna's work. My husband bought this painting for me for when we moved into this house (during the design phase, we had created a special spot for it to hang proudly.) Later, Donna and I met, and we are still in touch. Her daughter interned in my office for a summer.

   Purely from a design standpoint, it is critical to place works of art and collections strategically. If the decision is to stack the artworks, then stack them. Grouping like objects together can draw the eye and heighten their impact. Random arrangements do little for the individual pieces and even less for the overall room. My rule for placement is straightforward: the eye naturally moves across the room within a definite range of heights. That comfort zone remains fairly constant whether we're standing or sitting, so I try to place all the major elements and art pieces within it. Finding that level is key. If the heights are too widely varied—if there is too much up and down—the eye has to work too hard and registers only clutter and confusion.

*Above: Classic sterling silver picture frames with family photos decorate the antique table behind the living room sofa. Facing, clockwise from upper left: My Herend figurines reflect my love of animals; this painting is a memento of a family visit to Italy; the shells that fill the centerpiece are a mix of those collected along our beach and ones Rick brought back from Africa; I purchased this antique book of watercolors when I was working on the Melrose Inn.*

To create a feeling of coziness in our open dining room, I designed these high-backed banquettes to embrace the table. From my line, *J Banks Collection by Stanford Furniture*, these upholstered chairs are crafted for comfort and encourage us to linger after the meal. The dining room table calls for a centerpiece. For everyday purposes and practical beauty, I often fill ours with shells collected from our beach and our travels.

*Above: Silver accessories are true to southern tradition. Our dining room sideboard, which I found on a trip to England, holds classic silver frames with family photos and a silver tureen with garden flowers. Facing: Linen textiles offer elegance without pretense, a hallmark of our coastal lifestyle.*

*Previous overleaf: I wanted the family room to feel as if it were wrapping us in its embrace, so it has a larger fireplace, fewer windows, and a color palette that is deeper hued and warmer toned than in our other rooms. Above and facing: Because we gather here as a family and the girls often have their friends over to watch a movie, the furnishings are designed for lounging and sprawling.*

*Facing: I draped the windows of the family room so that we could filter daylight and the night's reflections as necessary. The walls are finished to resemble plaster in a shade of ochre that recalls our times in Italy. Above: Tulips in a silver cup bring the warmth of the palette into the room's core.*

*Facing: Many of the textiles in the family room are from my fabric collection for Kravet,
with patterns inspired by our trips to Africa. Because these fabrics are for use in both
home and hospitality settings, they are incredibly durable—and perfect when you have pets
like Daisy, above, who loves to lounge on the upholstery.*

# MY COLOR THEORIES

Color is culture, geography, emotion, memory, atmosphere, and so much more. People react to color viscerally. That is why color is one of design's most powerful tools, and arguably its most mysterious, personal, and complex.

Even when I begin to believe that I understand all the nuances of color, it continues to teach me new lessons. One year, for example, the organizers of Maison & Objet in Paris—an annual French trade show for furnishings and decorative arts—put together a fascinating exhibition on the art and science of this most impactful element of design. It consisted of an installation of a series of small rooms, each done entirely in one hue—tables, chairs, walls, dishes, everything. One room was all white; another, blue; yet another, green, etc. As we stepped into each room, we were to assess how we felt in the world of that hue. The organizers monitored our physical responses—heart rate, breathing, that sort of thing—as we moved from room to room. The data reinforced what many of us knew instinctively: the spectrum is a physiological and psychological trigger.

Working in different countries and climates has taught me how much heritage and environment can unconsciously influence our color preferences. In my experience, people from northern European countries tend to prefer cooler colors, while those from the southern Mediterranean areas almost invariably prefer the warm tones. This seems to hold true no matter where in the world they live. We Americans, too, follow our instincts and cultural bents. In our sunnier regions, when we don't choose snowy white, we often opt for more saturated, brighter, and warmer hues than we would in a cooler climate. By the same token, rooms along both coasts feel and look completely at home in the blues and whites of the nearby beach. Some palettes seem to suit urban living to a tee, while others seem naturally appropriate for mountain and lakeside homes.

Here is another perplexing truth: color can, and does, change color depending on environmental factors. From one time of day to another, from one location to another—meaning surroundings, longitude, and latitude—the same color can seem to be a different hue entirely. The living room walls of my family home on Hilton Head Island exemplify that kind of changeability. When people ask me for the paint color, which is gray, I give them the paint chip. Their response, always, is, "No. I want your blue." Now, our house is right on the water, and our living room focuses on that view. We get a great deal of natural daylight, as well as reflected light off the water. Because of where we are, and the quality of light that fills the room over the course of the day, that gray reads as blue. At night, it becomes another color altogether. That's why I always advocate adapting the palette to the place as well as the person.

*So many influences affect our palette preferences. For years, I traveled regularly to Italy to work on our hotel project Castello di Casole. Often, my family joined me there. That experience comes through vividly in the colors and finishes of our family room.*

*Facing: Our kitchen is the multifunctional heart of our house. Because it's the place where we gather every day as a family, and the room where we often host our extended family and friends, I thought through the design to the last detail. Above: The kitchen counters often do duty as handy surfaces to set out appetizers and buffet meals.*

Our family dining area is a casual, very convenient bridge between the kitchen and the family room. Here, Rick, Grace, Sarah and I sit down to share a meal that we've made together. Covered in leather, the banquette stands up beautifully to the wear and tear of family life. A sawbuck table and comfortable yet quirky chairs complete this well-used gathering space.

*Above and facing: Whether it's an impromptu meal or a long-planned celebration,*
*we love to entertain at home. I'm a great believer that preparation makes everything easier.*
*For that reason we always have a variety of fun options for setting a pretty table close at*
*hand—and a well-stocked pantry.*

*Previous overleaf: We are fortunate to live right on the water, so we designed our house to embrace both the view and the environment. Above and facing: Living in such a temperate climate allows us to use our outdoor dining area for most of the year.*

# WORKING WITH ARTISANS

Design is in the details, especially when the details are made by hand and are absolutely unique. That is why I feel that one of my most important jobs is to search out talented artisans at home and wherever I travel; it also happens to be great fun and an interesting way to discover new people and places. Along with artwork, the pieces made by artisans insert a special layer of beauty into our rooms.

Ceramics, woven baskets, collected treasures that are made by hand with traditional techniques—often hundreds of years old and passed down from father to son, mother to daughter—are what I use to infuse a room with real glimpses of the owner's personality and life experience. The client and I consult closely on the artisanal elements. We have a vision in mind, and I work with the artisan to get it just right, as the artisan transforms the idea into reality. In that wonderful, mysterious process of design development and creation, the piece somehow takes on an aspect of its owner. As a result, the finished piece makes that room completely unlike any other.

We commissioned a local potter, for example, to make a powder room sink for one of our clients. He was able to show her various glazes and examples of bowls. She selected what she wanted, we measured her space for size, and he set to work. The sink is uniquely hers; there is not another like it in the world. She enjoyed the process so much that we commissioned other pieces, including a long bowl made from wine barrel staves for her kitchen countertop.

The kitchen is one of the rooms where we often use artisan-made pieces. As the countertops and islands get larger and larger, it becomes more difficult to find distinctive ready-made pieces in the correct scale. So we work with artisans and craftspeople who will make bowls, ceramics, wood artifacts, candles—you name it—in sizes that are substantial enough to fill these spaces. On my own kitchen island, I have a collection of overscaled candles as well as large bowls and platters that I fill with fruit or vegetables—perfectly useful and absolutely unique.

In instances when the entire family gets involved in the process of choosing or commissioning pieces by artisans, those pieces feel appropriate to their family life. There are many different ways to edit the selection process. One way is by theme. Another way is to choose the piece with variety in mind, or to add color to the house. Above all, I think an artisan piece should evoke some kind of emotion or memory. That way, it will always be special.

*I am always on the lookout for talented artisans and skilled craftspeople who tend to the legacy of traditional techniques. Things that are made by hand—especially those commissioned for a particular space—add the touches of uniqueness that can transform a very pretty home into a profound personal expression.*

# Coastal Glamour

The designers who work with me believe as I do, that the homes we create should reflect the personalities of their owners, suit the architectural vernacular of the house, and capture the spirit of their geography and surroundings. I think our southern coastal style welcomes the widest possible range of looks for those very reasons. With its sophisticated European details and relaxed plan, this house attests to the variety and individuality our approach delivers.

Designer Sharon Cleland took the lead with this client, a busy young public relations executive who purchased the home to serve as the primary residence for herself and her young child. The client wanted it to be casual, family friendly, and conducive to hosting guests because she entertains often and her relatives visit regularly from England. She also asked that the house reflect the Lowcountry lifestyle while expressing her eclectic tastes.

Sharon explained, "I always tell clients that I want the home to exude their soul. That means that we make sure to fill it with treasures that they connect with, elements that show off their personality, travels, and passions. She likes to mix funky with traditional, and antique with modern, as do I. She was wonderful to work with because she has so many passions and different interests, and travels so diversely."

Because the house had been standing empty for several years, it was in need of a total renovation. The process began with the public spaces that are the heart of every house: the kitchen, family room, living room, and Carolina room (our vernacular term for sunroom). Our client opted to keep all existing kitchen cabinets and built-ins, upgrading them with a new finish. In the Carolina room, Sharon incorporated some of her existing furniture pieces. She and the client shopped for antiques and rugs at Scott's Antique Market in Atlanta. A number of pieces, including the demilune in the foyer and the center table in the master bath, are fine reproductions made by one of our wonderful vendors in Italy.

*To create a family-friendly home for a client with sophisticated, eclectic style, we mixed antiques with modern pieces and layered in the velvets and silks that suit her English upbringing but that are not typically used in Lowcountry interiors.*

Blue and white are predominant in the palette, yet the array of blues ventures into unexpected territory with both pale shades and dark indigos. Sharon explains that "the blue palette continues throughout the house, but we also wanted some other punches of color. In the Carolina room, we brought in richer, warmer colors and the grasscloth wallcovering, which we also used in the back of the bookcases in the family room."

Typical Lowcountry emblems, such as the silver pheasants in the foyer, layer these rooms with references to place. In the dining room are an oyster-shell light fixture, a driftwood finish on the dining table, and nubby linen fabric on the chairs. These same items also introduce organic elements into the house naturally and beautifully.

The velvets in the living room and the silks in the master bedroom, on the other hand, might be considered anomalous to our regional design vocabulary. They suit the client's very English tastes, however, as well as Sharon's Irish background. "It was interesting to work with someone who comes from the same part of the world as I do," says Sharon, "and to bring in textures and fabrics and a little bit more of that traditional European style that I would have been more comfortable using in Ireland. Typically, I do not use those here."

The master bathroom, the most private space of all, epitomizes the mix of influences, elements, and finishes that characterize these interiors. After completely gutting the existing bath, we created a uniquely glamorous and very personal retreat. "She's very open to mixing finishes," says Sharon. This led to a blend that I think is quite singularly glamorous for a house on Hilton Head Island: gold with shiny chrome, stains with painted finishes, and antique woven rugs with fine furniture.

The art throughout the house is among its most strikingly personal elements. An artist friend of the client's from California painted the contemporary works in the living room, the stairway, and the master bedroom and bathroom. Because of their close relationship, we based many of our schemes around these wonderful works.

*Seagrass wallcovering provides a wonderfully effective neutral background for art.*
*Here, we've hung a collection of figure drawings in a symmetrical grouping for greater impact.*
*The blue corals add notes of coastal texture and color.*

*The oyster shell fixture hanging above the
dining table is a classic element of Lowcountry
décor. In combination with the table's driftwood
finish, the textured linens, and the elegantly
rustic seagrass rug, it introduces the organic into
the room in a sophisticated way.*

*Above: The classic coastal color scheme of blue and white with neutrals offers designers endless variety—and endless pleasure. Facing: The foyer's reproduction demilune sideboard, handcrafted to look like an original antique, is topped with a pair of silver pheasants, a typical southern emblem. The contemporary artwork, painted by one of her friends, influenced the design scheme.*

# EDITING

We can only absorb so much visual information at any given time. That is why editing—separating the necessary from the unnecessary—is essential to good design.

Editing is now second nature to me, but this was not always the case. When I was just getting started professionally, I was fortunate enough to work with the late William Frank McCall, who was famous then for his southern architecture and resort interiors. The project was the Melrose Inn. I was taken by the fact that he could walk through a space and make decisions so easily. I had to look through books and magazines and play the slideshow in my mind before determining what to do. On that project, I needed help with the design details of the bar shelves in the dining room and parts of the veranda. Mr. McCall knew instantly what to do. I set my goal then to hone this skill and come to a point in my career where I, too, would know immediately, so that I could spend my contemplation time on the impactful details.

I am sure that living on Hilton Head Island has contributed greatly to my understanding of the true power of editing. Here, every detail has been thought out from an aesthetic standpoint. I was privileged to work closely with the Frasers, who developed Hilton Head and spent time explaining the process. Mr. Fraser traveled **widely** and took photos everywhere he went. **Then** he compiled all the elements for Hilton Head—the covenants, the zoning restrictions, all the constructed elements, down to the mailboxes and bicycle stands—to create what we who live here consider a practically perfect environment.

My focus as a designer is always on curating the elements to create engaging, bespoke homes that express the people who occupy them. With any given room, I start by defining the focal points, those places where I want people to look when they enter. As I begin developing the scheme, with every choice I make I am constantly assessing scale, proportion, and details. Once my scheme is clear, I lay out everything I like for the given project so that I can see it all together. Then I start removing the elements that seem extraneous. Because the process of design takes time, the challenge is to stay true to the original vision so that the rooms develop character but keep their essential identity, and provide the sense of place I initially conceptualized.

I believe some people work from details up to big picture, and some people work from big picture down to details. The best designers are able to transition fluidly between the two ends of the spectrum. All of that effort—and editing—is directed toward realizing the client's vision. For that, everyone involved has to trust in each other and in their own instincts.

If a client really loves a particular piece, even one that is far from the preferred style as stated, I need to consider it and find a way to work it into the overall scheme. It is my responsibility as a designer to explore what my clients want and what they instinctively love so that I can bridge any divide that may exist. Editing is the process I use for that purpose.

*In every home, we explore what the clients want and what they instinctively love. Then we find a way to bring cohesion and clarity to the mix. This balancing act—the process of editing—is what we use to bring that family's unique vision into focus.*

Great Escapes Europe

*The* FRENCH WAY *with* DESIGN        PHILLIPS

LARS BOLANDER        INTERIOR DESIGN & INSPIRATION

MAKING ASTON MARTIN        Ulrich Bez

RANKIN        SPIRIT OF ECSTASY

*Above: The master suite is a serene getaway in ice blue, cream, and neutrals. Facing: We furnished the master bath as a private retreat for daily pampering and recharging. The custom-made standing Venetian mirror provides a focal point for the room; behind it are his and hers showers.*

In the master suite, we elaborated on the eclectic mix that this client prefers. Here, an antique chaise joins custom and contemporary pieces and a vibrant painting from her collection to achieve the desired effect.

# SHINING MOMENTS

Reflective surfaces, gleaming finishes, and tantalizing flickers are very important components of design and entertaining, both inside and outdoors. These details—candles, flatware and accessories in silver and other metals, and mirrors—are what I often use to create a little home magic. They can set a scene, change a mood, and enhance an atmosphere. Apart from their function and decorative impact, each introduces a special, indefinable something to a tabletop, a vignette, a wall, a display grouping. They attract and delight the eye.

When I started my career as a designer, it was the era of the mirrored wall—a much more formal time. We would frequently dress at least one of the room's vertical surfaces in a reflective finish from floor to ceiling, from one end to the other. Those mirrored walls helped us solve a myriad of spatial issues, and their effect was always wonderfully dramatic. They may be passé now, and not much missed, but they taught me a great deal about how to direct the eye around a room's perimeter and through its interior.

There is still a significant place for mirrors in today's design language—large standing mirrors and well-placed hanging mirrors in particular. With a tall mirror in the middle of the wall or a large cheval glass, it is possible to totally change the perceived scale of a room. Mirrors play with the light, the view, and the texture within a room. They can redirect the eye between the room's various focal points and connect the room to the surrounding landscape by bringing an exterior view deep into the interior. I may use a tall standing mirror along a very long wall to interrupt the length. And any mirror will set light dancing at all hours of the day and into the night.

*Reflective and gleaming surfaces, such as this master suite's antique mirror, nailhead trim, burnished hardware, and silvered finishes, will set light in motion through a space, which is why I feel they can create a magical effect in a room.*

*Above: The Venetian mirror reflects back highlights of this master bath. Facing: The mirrored vanity speaks to her style and helps the light to dance throughout the space. Overleaf: The silk damasks and embroideries of her English upbringing blend with elegant rustic textures.*

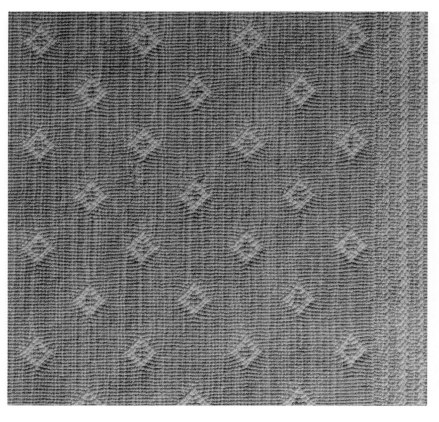

*Left: Our client encouraged us to mix finishes. Here the burnished gold of the hardware complements the lustrous silk curtain panels and silver-leafed moldings. Above: The graceful forms in the figure sketch echo the curves of the chair. Facing: In the master bath, we wanted to make the old fit with the new. A reproduction claw-footed tub sits under the eave.*

# Guest Rooms

Banks Design specializes, somewhat unusually, in both residential and hospitality design. I find that the two areas of expertise influence each other in many ways. In my experience, this is particularly the case for the master suite and the guest room, where hospitality design truly comes home.

Hospitality is the gift of making people feel as truly welcome and cared for as they do at home—and even more so. When family and friends come to visit for an overnight or longer, it is so nice to provide them with all the essentials for a happy, memorable stay, and some thoughtful luxuries too. The world's great resorts and hotels do that as a matter of course, which is where I believe this crossover story starts.

In a guest room, as elsewhere, thinking about how the space is meant to function helps me to determine what furnishings and accessories to include. Beside the bed, I always make sure to have a place to set a glass and a bottle or carafe of water. I want people to feel comfortable using it, so I'll make sure there is a coaster or something comparable handy. When possible, a bedside component that is large enough to accommodate a reading lamp, a guest's reading glasses, a book, and even a box of tissues makes the room feel homey. Optimally, the bottom of the lampshade or wall sconce should be 20 inches above the bedside table or mattress.

Fabulous bed linens make all the difference to any guest's feeling of being welcome and comfortable, whether in a home or a hotel. In fact, most of us have our first encounters with high-quality bedding and beautiful baths when we travel and experience the unique luxuries that the world's fine hotels and resorts have to offer. After staying in these wonderful getaways, it feels only right to bring back some memento of our time there. Those linens—the crisp white sheets and duvet covers, the wonderful towels—are what many of us translate easily into our homes. The beautiful materials used so elegantly in hotel baths—the marbles and granites, the ceramic tiles and mosaics, the faucets and fittings—often inspire what my clients ask for when they're planning a renovation, building an addition, or constructing a new home.

*Residential design and hospitality design—my firm's two areas of expertise—have many crossover influences. Hospitality design truly comes home in the guest room, where the function of the space helps me edit the selection of furnishings and accessories.*

*Facing: The guest room's bedside components should be ample enough to accommodate reading material and a lamp. Above: A windowed niche with a freestanding bathtub creates a perfect spot for a long, luxurious soak.*

A comfortable chair or chaise is always welcome in a guest room, and proper storage accoutrements are imperative. A luggage rack, I find, is a must, because there are many people who choose not to unpack fully during their stay. For those who do, it is important to provide them with enough hangers in the closet. Additionally, a dresser or chest of drawers is always gracious.

In the bath, hanging a robe strikes a very thoughtful note. I will also make sure that the daily essentials are close at hand: a hairdryer, shampoo and conditioner, soaps, toothpaste and extra toothbrushes, razors. That way they don't feel they have to bring all their toiletries with them; if they do and happen to have forgotten something, you've already got it covered.

Finally, there are the little touches. Fresh flowers say a warm hello immediately and make your guests feel that you're excited to see them. And putting out a book or a magazine that's current, and that you've enjoyed, is another wonderful way of sharing your thoughts.

*Above and facing: Proper storage accoutrements are imperative in a guest room. For guests who want to unpack their suitcases, roomy drawers will allow them to organize their things as if they were at home. Overleaf: When the details of a guest room show consideration for a guest's comforts, the guest feels warmly welcomed.*

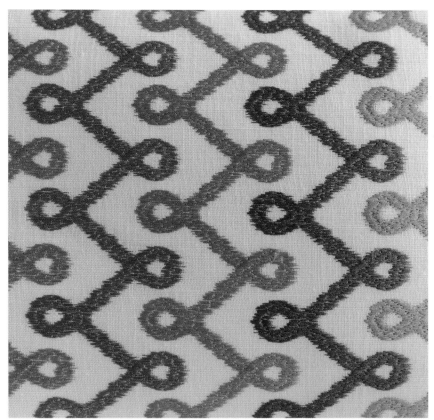

*Facing and above: The luxurious materials, elegant fixtures, and sophisticated fittings that my clients encounter when they stay in fine hotels and resorts often inspire them when they're planning a bath renovation, a guest room addition with an en suite bath, or a new home.*

*Above and facing: Fabulous fresh bed linens—especially crisp white sheets, wonderful duvets, and luxurious pillows—
make all the difference to making a guest feel wanted, comfortable, and cared for, whether in a home or a hotel.*

*Facing and above: Providing furnishings, spaces, and time for guests to relax and feel pampered will create pleasant memories of their stay with you.*

*Above: I always make sure to have a place to set a glass and a bottle or carafe of water by the bed.*
*Facing: Putting out a book that you've read and enjoyed is a fine way to share your thoughts. Fresh flowers always make guests feel that you're happy to see them.*

# DRESSING THE BED

Among life's truly great comforts, there are few things more wonderful than a beautifully made bed. There is a correct way to dress a bed: layering the elements up from the ground, with the dust ruffle as the starting point.

There are two options for a dust ruffle: an overlay that covers the box spring, or panels secured by upholstery hooks. It is easier to launder panels and also to adjust them for proper length. The dust ruffle should skim the floor, rather like the proper drape of a man's trousers. To maintain the correct "hang" of the dust ruffle, follow the laundering specifications exactly to ensure that the fabric does not shrink, stretch, etc. Upholstery hooks are great to mistake-proof this step; if the fabric does shrink, stretch, or change shape, the hooks can be adjusted as necessary.

Next come the sheets. For comfort and longevity, I recommend high-quality linens, 400 thread count or higher. I layer them as follows: fitted sheet, flat sheet facing down, blanket, flat sheet or blanket cover facing up. The flat sheet must face down so that when the linens are folded over, the finished side faces up; this arrangement also decreases the frequency with which a blanket needs laundering. (The blanket cover, traditionally called a night spread, decorates the bed when the bedspread is removed. Night spreads are designed to fall to the bottom of the mattress, so that they cover the blanket and bed sheets, for a finished look. Matelassés are great for this purpose.

Bedspreads and coverlets provide the next layer. The primary difference between a bedspread and a coverlet is coverage. A bedspread generally covers the entire bed, going up over the pillows and draping down to the floor. A coverlet tends to be smaller, just covering the top of the bed and dropping down barely past the box spring; for that reason, it is often accompanied by a bedskirt, unless the bed base is to be exposed, such as when a more contemporary look is required or a more austere look for a traditional bed is wanted.

Then there is the duvet. A duvet should be folded in thirds—like an "S"—so that when the bed's occupants pull the edge closest to them, the duvet easily covers the bed. Duvets should be placed button side down so the enclosure is not exposed. When allergies are not an issue, down inserts are preferable to synthetic blends.

Last, but far from least, are the pillows. The standard order for layering pillows is as follows (starting from the headboard): two sleeping pillows, two Euro shams, two decorative standard shams, and one additional decorative pillow. All sham inserts should be down, not synthetic blends, unless allergies dictate otherwise.

*The proper way to dress a bed is to layer it from the ground up, starting from the dust ruffle and working up to the coverlet or duvet and, finally, the various pillows.*

*Above: A bed built into an alcove transforms an unconventional space with seating niches and unexpected nooks into a multifunctional room that can house an extra guest. Facing: In the confines of this narrow room under the eave, built-in bunk beds provide a perfect solution for visiting children.*

*Facing: Plush towels and other bath accoutrements elevate the everyday act of bathing to a new level of luxury. Above: With endless available options in marbles and granites, ceramic tiles, glass and stone mosaics, and vintage-inspired faucets and fittings, the bath offers tremendous possibilities for design invention.*

*Facing: The rugged rope-knot lamps and jute hassock balance this guest room's more refined materials in a wonderfully tactile way. Above: A well-curated collection of objects that capture the spirit of the region gives a guest bedroom an authentic sense of place.*

# Coastal Brights

Thanks to the mobility that digital technology provides, many people now work remotely and are free to choose where they wish to settle and raise their families. Among our clients are many such transplants to Hilton Head Island. As a rule, they generally have very clear ideas of not only the kind of lifestyle they envision but also how they want their homes to reflect and support it. This family of four is a wonderful example of that.

Hannah Fulton, lead designer on this project, explains, "These clients had lived many places, including in New York and overseas, before moving to Hilton Head. They came to us with their vision of a coastal home, one that would be very bright and full of vibrant color but not too beachy. They wanted a livable, approachable home where their family, including two young children, could be comfortable."

When they purchased the house about twelve years ago, it was rather dark. A major renovation that included removing a number of walls and all the dark-stained woods helped solve that problem. The addition of a children's wing with two bedrooms, three bathrooms, a laundry room, a kitchenette, an exercise room, and a craft room on the second story further shifted the house's center of gravity to family pursuits—and the wing can almost function independent of the main space. As Hannah says, "It really is a wonderful blend of design, beauty, and function. The children have violin lessons, tutoring, and all different kinds of activities, and they're able to do it all in that wing. They use every inch of it."

These clients loved white. They also loved the look of clean-lined Scandinavian pieces that are whitewashed or made of pale woods. What they wanted was to bring their personal touch to that concept through use of bright colors—their whimsical, inspiring palette of hot pinks, saturated turquoises, and brilliant yellows. Hannah reports that, quite unusually, "the husband was really active in the design decisions. I would present things to the couple and he would say, 'Let's go brighter!'"

Their kitchen truly is their home's beating heart. We built in a range of storage options, including a glass-fronted china cabinet, to make the tableware accessible for the children. Hannah says, "She has so many beautiful pieces, and it was wonderful to break up the white kitchen with all of her bright china. We also did turquoise and pink hardware

*In the family room, bold colors and bright white combine happily. The clients wanted to be able to relax here with their children without always having the TV as a focus, so we custom designed a large wall unit with a scissor lift for the TV.*

to give those pops of color that they were expecting and to tie in with the window treatments and upholstery pieces in the adjacent Carolina and family rooms that open off the kitchen and overlook the pool, deck, and golf course.

Fabric selection is always a critical aspect of our design process. That is certainly true in this house, where the mélange of textures—and especially the vibrant, custom-printed linens at the windows—contribute so much to the spirit of these living spaces. "The clients weren't really sold on window treatments, but in the end they loved them," says Hannah. "The side panels bring color to the vertical plane and also help connect and ground the high ceilings."

The children's rooms are very special and definitely worlds unto themselves. For their son, the clients specifically requested a nautical look—and a room that would last for years. It has. When Hannah started working on it, he was a toddler. Twelve years later, he loves the room just as much as ever. "The wallpaper sets the tone," says Hannah. "His bed is a custom piece made to look like a Chris-Craft boat. It has trundle beds that pull out from either side, storage at the base for extra linens, and a steering wheel, where he loved to sit when he was small."

*Above: Strong hues work beautifully together when they are well balanced in intensity.*
*Facing: We designed the kitchen built-ins to accommodate and display all her beautiful, brightly colored china and glassware—and to be easily accessible to the children.*

*Above: Drapery panels in vivid colors help make this family room feel light and airy. Facing: Raoul Textiles custom printed the vibrant linen drapery fabric. Overleaf: Along with the bright palette, the textures, patterns, finishes, and accessories factor into the visual balance.*

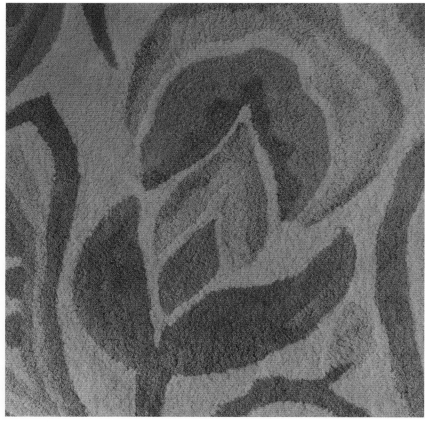

*Facing and above: This bedroom offers another version of the brights-with-white palette by emphasizing the cool tones with saturated shades of aqua and grass green and using the hot hues of pink, orange, and yellow—plus grounding black—as accents.*

For their son's room, they wanted a nautical theme that would last for years—and it has. The custom-made bed looks like a Chris-Craft and incorporates trundle beds that pull out from either side, storage for extra linens, and a steering wheel.

*Above and facing: The Ralph Lauren paper with the ships and the matching fabric on the lounge chair establish the nautical tone. Symbols from maritime signal flags incorporated into the rug border, the pillows, and the wall art contribute to the nautical theme of the room. The beadboard dado is a classic coastal element.*

# For Pete's Sake

Although Hilton Head Island is known for its golf courses, tennis courts, and water sports, the island and surrounding areas happen to be horse country, too. We have a number of clients with a passion for all things equestrian, but perhaps none more than the wife of this couple. Their primary residence is a beautiful oceanfront house on Hilton Head Island. This gem of a house in neighboring Palmetto Bluff is a getaway home, of sorts.

Here is the backstory: When she got her horse, Pete, years ago, she decided to paddock him at Palmetto Bluff, a 45-minute drive inland. She found herself spending far too much time in transit every day, so she and her husband thought it would be convenient to have a place she could use a few nights a week that was closer to Pete's stable. They found this property, which backs directly onto the corral. When she is in residence here and Pete is in the pasture, it is as if he's right in the backyard.

The couple named the house "For Pete's Sake." It was just in the framing stages when they began working on it with project designer Shelley Wilkins. Shelley and the wife started by going through the plans and upgrading every aspect, down to each finish and detail. The only element they were unable to change was the roof, because it was already in place. The wife loves the process of building and designing, says Shelley. "This client is absolutely so much fun to work with. She always includes so much detail in every little piece of the interior, which makes the process very interesting and enjoyable and elevates the design to another level."

While this home exhibits a relaxed, functional spirit, it has very refined appointments. In these rooms, new mixes with old: custom upholstered pieces for comfort blended with many antique furnishings and light fixtures. The palette of finishes celebrates the glow of highly polished materials—glossy patinas, various marbles, nickel and white bronze, as well as gold leaf on all the window hardware. Shelley says that she and the clients laugh now when they refer to the house as a farmhouse, "because it is definitely finer."

*On axis with the front door, an antique bronze of a jockey sits proudly on an antique English stone table on the porch. We placed it consciously so that the eye must travel through it to the pasture beyond.*

The house centers on the view. At the entry, one looks straight through the living room out to the screened porch and beyond to the green fields; for focus—and for psychological symmetry—the eye must go through a sculpture of a jockey atop a huge stone table on the porch to reach the pasture.

Opening off the living room are the kitchen and dining area, with a table that seats eight. Also on the main floor are a powder room, her office, and the master bedroom and bath.

Her office, which exudes her love of horses, shows off the powers of design. Both the windows and the ceiling are off center, a flaw that Shelley's clever planning has corrected. As she explains, "It was difficult to create a design that made sense in the room and lined up with the existing ceiling. The first thing we purchased was the painting of the horse with the orange hood. We developed the panel sizes of the room around the piece. Then we decided what panel the painting would hang on and laid out the rest of the room around it. We covered the ceiling with pecky cypress in a herringbone pattern, which helps disguise the fact that it doesn't line up properly with the windows. We also upholstered the walls and draped the windows with curtains that have a gorgeous embroidered edge. The client purchased a beautiful antique desk for the space. A small bronze horse sitting on a side table gives a nod to the reason the couple are here."

The palette for the home includes many shades of blue in both the public and private areas of the house. In the master bedroom, says Shelley, "the walls are a beautiful shade of gray-blue paint called Kentucky Haze, which we then accented with warmer colors, like camels and browns." The master bath is a serene retreat lined in white marble and graced with many unique touches, such as the antique mirror incorporated into the tub skirt and a de Gournay wallpaper, custom colored in select shades of gray and blue.

The herringbone pattern that Shelley used for her office ceiling repeats, subtly, in the brick design of the porch floors and the various walkways. The brick is Savannah Gray, which is appropriate for this area and adds texture and warmth.

*When we opted to use the house's formal dining room for another purpose, we enhanced the area off the kitchen for dining. The furnishings accommodate both casual and more formal meals.*

*Preceding overleaf: A refined rusticity prevails on the porch, where the view embraces the pool, the cabana, and the pasture. Above: Handily adjacent to the kitchen, the dining area centers on a table that seats eight. Facing: A convenient niche of the kitchen houses the bar beautifully.*

*Facing: Her office includes an antique writing desk. Drapery panels are embellished with embroidery; curtain rings and finials are finished in gold leaf. Above: This painting was the first piece purchased. Our enhancements to this room include the pecky cypress paneling. Overleaf: Each of the room's decorative choices reveals her passion for design and horses.*

*Above: They love animals but did not want a true mount above the bed. When we found this gold-plated piece, we thought it would be perfect. Facing: In one corner of the master suite, characterful antiques add form, function, and history.*

At the heart of the master bedroom is an upholstered walnut four-poster. The room's walls are
painted a shade of gray-blue called Kentucky Haze.
Accent colors include warm camels and browns.

*Facing and above: The master bath is a serene, elegant retreat done almost entirely in white,
with counters, backsplash, tub deck, and floors finished in delicately veined Calacatta marble.
On the walls is a de Gournay wallpaper custom colored in soft shades of grays and blues.*

# THE CABANA

There is a long tradition here in the South of "farm" properties that evolve over time. This couple's experience in Palmetto Bluff demonstrates how such domestic expansions continue to occur. When they finished the farmhouse, Shelley says that they found themselves envisioning a fuller daily experience when they were here on site. They purchased the lot to the right of them and started building the pool house, which everyone calls the cabana.

Essentially one big room, the cabana encompasses a kitchen and living area, plus a bathroom, porch, and the pool. It was designed for fun and easy durability. And although it features more rustic, less polished furnishings and finishes, it has a very defined elegance that suits the wife's design sensibility.

This couple has a pair of Middleburg Spaniels, Robey and Gus, that like to swim in the pool in the summer and then come back into the cabana and relax. Most of the upholstery in the cabana is upholstered in an indoor/outdoor fabric so the dogs can "hop up on the sofa and not hurt it," explains Shelley.

When this couple originally purchased this house—and even after they built the cabana—they thought they would only spend a couple of days a week here. But since moving in, they spend more time here—about four days a week—than in their oceanfront house because it is so peaceful and quiet. And they have decided to build a manor house on the other side of the cabana. Once that is finished, they plan to turn the farmhouse into a guesthouse. The cabana will stay the cabana, and when the manor house is complete, Shelley says, they will have a family compound.

*The cabana is essentially one big room that features a more rusticated but still elegant style. From the approach, one can look straight through the interior to the pool and pasture.*

*Above: In the cabana, all of the upholstery is covered with easy-to-maintain indoor/outdoor fabrics because the clients' two dogs love to swim in the pool and then come back inside to nap on the furnishings. Facing: Rugged wood ceiling beams, wide-plank wood floors, and a brick fireplace set the tone for the cabana's decor.*

The great hearth and mantel of the fireplace
serve as the secondary focal point for the
cabana's interior and the organizing
principle for a seating arrangement that
emphasizes comfort and conversation.

*Facing: In classic southern style, rocking chairs greet visitors to the cabana.*
*Above: The bricks are called Savannah Grays, so appropriate for this area.*
*Thin-set in a herringbone pattern, they add great texture and warmth.*
*Overleaf: The cabana opens to the back porch, pool, and paddock beyond.*

# A Classic
# Coastal Home

Occasionally, after doing a house for one family, they will move away and I will be asked to reinvent the same house in a completely different style for another family. When such a situation occurs, as it did here, it forcefully reminds me of what I love most about design: its powers of expression and transformation.

My history with this house, which is next door to ours, dates back to its conception. Family friends had purchased the property, and when they decided to build on it, they were inspired by the classically influenced designs of the great American architect Robert A.M. Stern. At that point, our friends also became my clients, so I was involved with every aspect of the home, from the interior plan and organization to the finishes, furnishings, and innumerable details.

One of the most important elements of the layout of this house—its sight lines—is also a key feature of our home and, I believe, of many southern homes. From the foyer, the eye travels straight through the house from front to back, where a wall of windows and French doors lead to various furnished porches and other outdoor living areas, including the pool. Functionally, this open style of interior planning encourages the flow of air through the interior. Emotionally, it incorporates the view as featured dramatic player in the life of the home. Physically, it both divides and joins the exterior and interior. (See entrance and center hall on page 6.)

From the first step inside, I will often mix materials and finishes that give subtle visual interest to the various surfaces and provide understated cues to help people focus and move through the house. In this foyer, for example, wood floors juxtapose with stone, a combination that I particularly like. This treatment breaks up the pattern of the architecture and also marks a significant intersection of the interior where a long hallway traverses the foyer.

As in our house, the bar is at one end of the foyer area and the kitchen at the other. This plan has proved to be a wonderful aid to entertaining, because guests can walk in and get their drinks and then move into the other parts of the home.

*Sight lines are a key feature in the planning of many southern coastal homes. Here, the symmetrical axial orientation of main house, pool, and pool house provides an organizing principle for the interior and exterior views.*

*Above: With stylish, comfortable lounge seating, the pool becomes its own outdoor room.*
*Facing: The glassed-in porch offers yet another spot for casual gatherings and impromtu enter-*
*taining, with contemporary wicker sectional seating upholstered in stylish, durable, indoor/*
*outdoor textiles that stand up beautifully to damp bathing suits and pets.*

When the original owners built this house, they wanted a very Scottish look—they have a home and roots in Scotland. Everything we did with the furnishings, fabric, palette, and accessories furthered that vision: imagine richer colors, such as deep greens, and plaids, and traditional antiques.

This family wasn't so certain about their preferred interior style at the outset. When they first moved in, they were living with the furniture they had brought from their previous residence. It was beautiful but far too traditional for the coastal look they ultimately decided was to their taste. We began to pore over images for concepts, and I showed them a few specific pieces of furniture and some fabrics that helped us edit our choices in a positive way. That got them focused, and the rest of our decisions proved to be smooth sailing.

This family is far more nautically inclined than the previous owners and loves the crisp combination of blues and white. So we decided to transform the house with paint and furnishings, keeping the finishes as they were. Our first steps involved painting the walls in the family room and living room a wonderful gray blue that reflects the colors of the exterior; this color changes throughout the day and from day to night, but it always feels as if it is bringing the outdoors inside and vice versa.

Although we made minimal architectural changes overall, we did close in what had been a screened porch. With its TV, this reinvented room provides yet another bright, comfortable living and entertaining space in a house full of them. Windows on two sides open to views of both the pool and the waterfront. The wicker furnishings give the room rich textural interest and provide a fantastic contrast with the crisp blue and white that dominates the palette here.

Their family room has that same indoor/outdoor quality and also reflects the view. Here we created a nautical look with caramel leather, caramel stripes, and a blue-and-white ticking stripe on the chair backs. The dining room, which was previously a very Scottish room with plaid-covered walls and dark green ceilings, is now all beautiful wood and nautical details, like the ship model over the mantel and the rope-and-glass globes that serve as the centerpiece.

All these rooms were beautiful in their previous state, but they didn't capture the personality of this particular family. Now they do. That's the power of design.

*This family has a nautical bent and loves the crisp combination of blues and white with neutrals and naturals. With tonal variations, we carried that color palette through all the areas of the home.*

*Facing: The blue-gray paint on the walls has a dynamic quality, changing character and hue with the available light and providing an atmospheric backdrop for the dark woods and caramel leather. Above: Succulents and potted herbs are practical, beautiful centerpieces that add life to the tabletop every day.*

Blue and white is an age-old match that remains endlessly fresh and pleasing to the eye. Depending on the materials, textures, and type of pattern, the combination can range in mood from rustic elegance to classic refinement to everything in between.

*Above: A touch of shine elevates a casual table setting. Facing: The glassed-in porch also incorporates an area for casual dining, making it a truly multifunctional area. Overleaf: In this dining nook, a consistent palette of blues and white creates a rich, nuanced harmony from many different patterns.*

# BLUE AND WHITE

In interior design and decorating, there are some matches that just seem made in heaven. In my opinion, blue and white is one of them—and to me, it also feels innately, classically southern. That could be because blue is the hue that we see most around us every day in our environment. Our southern skies are so often a bright, clear wash of aqua, interrupted only by white clouds that remind us of cotton. Many of us in this region also live close to the ocean, the sound, a lagoon, a lake, or a river.

Blue comes in an almost endless variety of tones, which our vistas show us so magnificently: indigo as the last light dies at sunset; cobalt in the lobelia just beyond the front door; the Wedgwood blue of hydrangeas and powder blue of early morning skies; the slate-tinged gray blue of the Atlantic in winter months.

Since blue is also on the cool end of the color spectrum, it does actually feel cooler to walk into a blue or blue-and-white room, especially when the temperature tops 100 degrees Fahrenheit on a sizzling hot summer day.

Blue-and-white accessories are very collectible and classic southern favorites. This makes sense, historically speaking: as our forebears sailed around the globe, they regularly brought back home the fine works they discovered abroad. Not least among them were the porcelains and ceramics in blue and white that now adorn so many of our historic houses. I have always found it fascinating that although the patterns differ, the palette itself unites cultures as far flung as the Chinese, French, Portuguese, Dutch, Danish, Japanese, and Moroccan, just to name a few.

Psychology indicates that blue surroundings allow the brain to become more creative, which suggests to me that the color also has a relaxing effect. In my experience, everyone responds quickly to blue-and-white fabrics in all sorts of patterns, from stripes to nautical themes, from nature views to geometrics and more. Our coastal clients very often prefer the combination of blue and white to any other. And that makes sense to me. In linen and cotton, blue-and-white designs look sharp. They are fresh, crisp, and clean and make a room feel bright and happy. One of my clients in Florida, in fact, has asked that I use blue and white, and only blue and white, in her homes—and I've now done that in the three I have designed. With her, I feel that I have used every blue-and-white fabric that exists.

*Facing: Ever since the ancients discovered pigments and dyes, the marriage of blue and white has been an enduring motif in the decorative arts. For many designers, myself included, the two remain a perfect pairing. Overleaf: From inky indigo to ice blue, from broad stripes to narrow bands, from intricate geometrics to complex florals, the range of possible hues and patterns is endless. Their juxtaposition also feels to me like a part of my southern heritage, perhaps because it ties us into this landscape of water and sky. Blue and caramel is another of my favorite combinations. Timeless and chic, it reminds me of seersucker, or my favorite pair of chambray ballet flats.*

Above: For the bedroom of a young man fascinated by all things nautical, we created a palette that combines deep ocean blues with natural and neutral shades in a variety of textures and materials. An antique map adds a layer of historical interest to the elements—and a compelling jolt of cobalt. Facing: The flag of the U.S. Yacht Ensign hangs over his bed, blanketed in mirroring stripes.

*Above: A breezeway connects this home's interior and exterior spaces. Facing: The covered terrace
extends this house's living spaces into the landscape, offering yet another exterior room with a gorgeous
view of the dock and Calibogue Sound for casual gatherings.*

# My Thoughts
# on Texture

nterior design is most successful for me when it activates and pleases all the senses. We respond to a design first with our eyes, of course, but the quality of touch is just as important. The relationship between the two is fascinating. As a designer, I know that the eye longs for elements that break up the continuity or sameness within our field of vision. For me, that ability to interrupt the continuity is texture's purpose and function. Think of it like this: if all the surfaces are slick, and all the fabrics as well, what is there to capture the interest of the eye? On the other hand, if there is a play of refined against rough, of smooth against coarse, of varying levels of fineness, the contrasts are compelling. They invite us to linger, and we do because we long to touch the various tactile components.

Seagrass, sisal, coir, wicker, rattan, wood—all are classic, organic textures in a southern home. Many of these plants grow along our coastal region. In the Lowcountry, craftspeople and artisans have worked with these materials for generations, plaiting and weaving them into beautiful baskets, floorcoverings, and other items for use around the household. Woven wicker furniture, for example, is almost a must-have in every southern home, in part because it adds such character. It is also very durable, practical, and casually elegant. Wonderfully cool to the touch, it has long been a staple choice for furnishing porches and verandas. In the South, however, we don't use wicker just for the exterior. It is also a traditional option in the dayrooms and morning rooms that are typical of southern houses.

Texture is as varied in its way as color, and texture has just as much charm and charisma. I find that small instances of pronounced textural elements add personality to a room—for instance, a chair with dimensional carving, e.g, a spool chair. I might include a chair with a woven back, especially on a porch. On occasion, I might place a carved or woven end table on one side of the room and comparably textured chairs on the other. The pairing adds an interesting character. It also evokes memories of a lifestyle of a past era, when the aesthetic was more rusticated and people lived with furnishings that were carved by hand.

*One of texture's functions is to interrupt—but not disrupt—visual continuity. A compelling contrast of refined against rough, of smooth against coarse, invites us to put our hands on the various components.*

Fabrics with texture are inviting. I love to watch people walk into a room, look at the available seats, and decide where they want to sit based on color, texture, and seat height. It is an interesting psychological study, and texture has something to do with how they make that choice. A textural fabric is cozier, and it is certainly more durable.

Accessories, along with pottery, baskets, and other textured items, draw the eye and shift its focus in close. Not only do accessories enhance the visual experience of the room but they also add character to it—and when these items are made by hand, they add another dimension entirely.

*Above: Dried mushrooms in a handmade ceramic dish reveal one of nature's own remarkable textural inventions. Facing: In a room where the tonal balance is consciously muted, a juxtaposition of natural and man-made materials draws the eye and invites the touch of the hand.*

*Facing: Rattan, wood, linen, and other natural fibers are classic options for materials in Lowcountry interiors. In this dining nook, one possible variation on the theme of polished versus organic is expressed. Above: Through contrast, an elegant leather basket filled with potted herbs and flowering plants highlights the refined finish of the wood tabletop.*

*Above: In a corner of this Carolina room, an appealing play of natural textures creates visual interest. Facing: Seagrass wallcovering, caned-back chairs, a wicker fan overhead, and sisal flooring combine in a beautiful balance of tactility that relates the interior design to the exterior landscape.*

# Kitchens

For most of us today, the kitchen is the heart of house. Instead of an appliance-filled, white, utilitarian space behind closed doors, it has become part of the living space, with its own distinctive look. In so many of our homes, it is truly that one space with everything a family needs to support their everyday life. This is partly because the kitchen's function has expanded to encompass family dining. Larger islands have created communal space for all sorts of activities, including food preparation. Barstools around the island turn it into a place for casual dining and other pursuits, as very often there will be a computer, television, or tablet on the work surface. I find that in the homes my designers and I work in now, 99 percent of the kitchens connect to a family room/living room of some type, which means that the family can be together while meal preparation is underway.

The evolution in the way we entertain over the last decade or two has also affected the design of kitchens quite profoundly. Many of our clients now tend to cook when the guests arrive. Everyone gathers in the kitchen until the preparations are done. In that role, the kitchen serves also as another living room—not just a working space or for family only—where design and decoration matter.

Because kitchens have changed, so has the way we approach kitchen design. We spend a tremendous amount of time at the beginning of each project determining just how the client wants the kitchen to function. We consider the storage needs, cabinet styles and finishes, hood, appliances, and the various surface materials. We analyze down to the decorative lighting and the last detail of the hardware just how each and every element fits into the space and furthers its function and beauty. We constantly consider the overall mix of materials and

*As the function of the kitchen has expanded to include family activities, its design has evolved. Frequently, it is the one space in the house furnished with everything a household needs for everyday family life—and the beautiful materials to match.*

*A larger island provides communal space for all sorts of activities that are food and family related. The addition of barstools transforms it into a place for casual dining and informal gathering during meal preparation.*

styles, just as for other rooms. We explore what the client prefers in every aspect of the space: for the styles and finishes on the cabinets and possibly within the cabinets, the countertops, and the hardware. We look at whether a combination of disparate elements creates the desired look, or whether the client prefers the harmonious space achieved by taking a unified approach. We talk through the possibilities for flooring in terms of function, comfort, and visual balance with the rest of the house.

I believe that cooking shows have changed the kitchen, and, more important, how we cook at home. More men cook now, as do more teenagers and children. The mother is no longer alone in the kitchen, but there are more likely to be two or three family members working together in the same space.

*The process involved in designing a kitchen is very analytical. Once it is clear how the space and the areas adjacent to it are intended to function, then it becomes possible to select the individual elements—cabinets, hood, appliances, surface materials, lighting, hardware, and furnishings.*

*The vast majority of kitchens in today's homes open directly to a family room/living room/dining area of some type so that the family can gather close at hand during meal preparation.*

# LIGHT TOUCHES

Human beings naturally turn to the light because it represents life and safety. Our desire and need for light is a primal instinct. Perhaps that is why I love rooms with pools of light. I feel that those areas of bright warmth in a room beckon to us and draw us in from the darkness in ways unlike any other element of design.

For me, a house without lamps is not finished. Well-chosen, well-placed lighting is a critical factor in establishing physical and emotional comfort in a room. Yet beyond the essential function of helping us to see, lamps create atmosphere and set mood.

I believe that the basic look of different light fixtures—floor, wall, and table, as well as chandeliers—can actually make or break a room. The scale, proportion, and texture of light fixtures directly affect the balance of a room's other elements, from the architectural envelope to the furniture arrangements to the art and accessories. Their style, materials, degree and quality of ornament are just as significant, because they factor into the harmonious expression of an interior's overall character, personality, and feeling.

There is a point in the editing process when the major elements of a space are practically set and determined—when the floor plan is in place, the furniture and fabrics selected (for the most part), and the overall palette decided. That is when the next phase of design questions begins. I will ask myself if the room has enough texture, if it needs more texture, if I need to create contrast between the room's paler and darker components, if there is a particular finish that I am trying to pull from one side of the room to the other. Whatever it may be that the room lacks at that stage of the layering process, a well-chosen lamp can very often supply.

One of the reasons my interiors have so many different types of lamps—and so many unusual ones—is because my designers and I work all over the country and all around the world. Those travels and experiences have broadened our understanding and expectations of design. They have also introduced us to many interesting people, great craft traditions, and countless wonderful resources. From Guadalajara to Tuscany and beyond, we have found talented artisans, vendors, and suppliers who are creating beautiful, unexpected, special pieces.

Much as I believe there are no hard-and-fast rules of design, there are some standard guidelines with lighting. The lowest festoon, arm, or drop of a dining room chandelier should hang 29 inches off the table. There are exceptions that call for a height or length adjustment, such as when the design and scale of a fixture do not make visual sense at that height in the way they relate to the room's proportions. Sconces, which tend to be more formal, present the same issues of scale: depending on their shape, there is an appropriate height for placing them in the room. Lamps for bedside reading are best when they are 20 to 24 inches from the top of the mattress to the bottom of the shade.

*Proper lighting is absolutely essential to an interior's overall look and balance. Beyond the essential function of illumination, each fixture's decorative style, design, and material contribute to the overall success of each room.*

The kitchen has evolved from a utilitarian work-
space into a multifunctional room for family living
and casual entertaining—the heart of the house. As
such, it has become an area where design and
decoration are essential.

*Above: In the kitchen, as in other rooms, we think through the design elements and overall mix of materials to find what best suits the client's needs and personality. Sometimes, the client prefers a palette of materials unified by consistent color. Facing page: Sometimes, more disparate elements create the desired look.*

*Above: Overhead fixtures provide focused, functional light to the work surface. Facing: Because my designers and I travel constantly, we encounter artisans, craftspeople, and vendors who make exceptional pieces. These opportunities allow us to commission or find unusual lighting fixtures that help make a room distinctive.*

# Men's Spaces

am so intrigued by men's spaces, or man caves, if you will. In almost every home that we do now, the men want one room that is their own designated domain: a place where they can get away to, concentrate, watch a football game. They always want these personal spaces to reflect their interests: golf, boats and the nautical life, travel, whatever it may be. Part of the fun for me is pulling that information out of them. Watching them settle in once the rooms are complete is such a pleasure. They really use their rooms. Usually, they cannot wait to show off their space to their friends and visiting family members.

I have found that in men's spaces, wood is particularly important. Men seem to truly love beautiful woods, especially when it is stained in rich, dark shades. They also love texture. In my experience, they also have an eye for items that show the touch of the hand—pieces that may not be quite as finely finished or as perfect as those we would use elsewhere in the home. Once the essential elements are in place, the challenge lies in finding or creating those pieces—whether whimsical or pertaining to a special interest—that express their character, reflect their personality, and capture their passion.

My husband, Rick, has his special place at the top of our house, overlooking the water, just off the area where Sarah and Grace do all their art, craft, and sewing projects. We've filled it with items that reflect his passions for hunting, fishing, and Africa—including the antique maps of Africa that I collect for him. We concentrate primarily on East Africa, which is our particular area of interest. The old maps are fascinating, in part because it took such a long time to map the entire continent, and in part because the boundaries of the countries have changed so much over the centuries. His maps document the transitions of colonialism, as well as the eras before and after. Each is different and has its own history. I've been able to find them at auctions, which I love. Because Rick is a doctor, my stepmother

*Men often prefer wood—beautifully grained, stained in rich, dark shades—for their personal spaces.*
*They also tend to love more rugged textures and items that show the hand that made them.*

*Once the essential elements of a man's room are in place, the challenge comes in finding or creating the specific pieces that express his character, reflect his personality, and capture his passions.*

searches out a gift each Christmas that is related to medicine; she is the force behind his collection of antique medical bags. His fishing gear is handy, as are his hunting trophies. It truly is a man's space.

Men also love having their own bars. They are great areas for people to congregate at a party. They are also terrific spaces for displaying the sports paraphernalia and other special items that so many men collect. In ours, we have a trophy from when my father's car won the very first race ever at Talladega. Apart from that, it is really Rick's world, full of his special things. He grew up in Boston, where his parents and brother still live, so he is a diehard Red Sox fan. Our girls, who grew up going to games at Fenway Park, are as well.

*Facing: Bars are classic men's spaces and offer natural spots for guests to congregate during parties. Above: They are also are wonderful places to display the sports paraphernalia and other special items that so many men collect. Overleaf: Rick's home office is like a treasure map of his passions. He always has his fishing gear close at hand. Because of his many medical missions to Africa and our family's efforts there, I have nurtured a growing collection of antique maps of the continent. He also cherishes a collection of antique medical bags, which my stepmother began for him and to which she adds each Christmas.*

*Facing and above: Men will ask for one room that belongs just to them, a place where
they can retreat, work, and focus on their interests. The gear from these interests often becomes
a part of the room's décor. Once they settle into these spaces, they really use them.*

*Above and facing: In my experience, men love spaces with distinctive textures, more rusticated finishes, and more rugged materials than those we might choose to use in a home's other rooms. They also seem to have an eye for items where the craftsmanship is visible.*

*Above and facing: In a shared master bath, I find it most conducive to balance the masculine and feminine influences in the palette of colors, materials, and accessories. The master suite in our home is one of the few areas where Rick wanted to be involved in those decisions.*

# Our Indoor/Outdoor Lifestyle

We are so very fortunate with our climate in the South, especially along the coast, which permits us a relaxed, indoor/outdoor lifestyle that brings us into nature on a daily basis. Many native species of flora and fauna flourish in this part of the country, where gardens are the passion of many. Our harbors and the ocean are so full of bounty and beauty. On Hilton Head Island, where development is planned and much of the land protected, our indigenous wildlife has a safe home. How we interact with the outdoors, how we extend our living and entertaining spaces beyond the walls of our houses, how we ease ourselves into the landscape are questions my designers and I think through with every home that we work on, including our own.

We have a long tradition in the South of porches, verandas, and patios, the "rooms"—covered or open to the sky, screened or glassed in, extending from the front, sides, and/or back of a house—where we daily spend time. When I began working as a designer, I could furnish a porch with a few rocking chairs and that would do. No longer. In recent years, these exposed spaces for dining and entertaining have become far more significant to the design of a home than they were even just a decade ago—and far more various. Now people want a grill area, a pool and pool house, an outdoor kitchen, an outdoor fireplace, a fire pit, and even a dock if they happen to be on the water. These amenities are now usual in new construction. For people with existing homes, we're finding ways to enhance and add to the exterior spaces that they already have to broaden their options out-of-doors.

Because we spend so much time on our porches, I prefer to think of them as additional living rooms. I design them accordingly, with furnishings that are stylish and comfortable and that carry the style and palette of the interior outside. On our porch, for example, which opens directly off the living room, we can make a cozy seating area for four, or open it up easily with pull-up chairs to accommodate six or eight. The ottomans allow us to expand the options further, and the swing—well, it's a hit with everyone who visits, especially in August! For accessories, we have collections of everything we find out on the beach, from shells and driftwood to sea glass and other items that wash in with the tide.

*A traditional part of our coastal architectural vernacular, the porch is an archetypal indoor/outdoor room that bridges the interior and exterior. Overleaf: A poolside terrace offers full sun; steps away, the veranda provides more cover.*

Just outside our family room, we have an outdoor cooking and grilling area with a Big Green Egg, coolers, and a refrigerator. We use it all the time, even in the winter months. When we're using the Big Green Egg, which we do often, even though we have a grill on our cooktop inside, we'll sit at the picnic table and keep the chef—Rick!—company. We grow herbs, lettuces, and vegetables in a bed around the corner from the grilling area. Well into the late fall, we have plenty of basil, rosemary, dill, cilantro, and parsley.

We also are blessed to have our beach and the dock, which is where we spend most of our time in the summer. We'll eat out on the dock, read books there, and gather with our family and friends for a Lowcountry boil. The dock is the one place that reliably catches a breeze on most summer days, so it's our outdoor "room" of choice. The whole family will take out the paddleboards, and our dogs, who love the water, will jump in wearing their life vests and swim alongside us.

*Above: With windows wide to catch the breeze, a glassed-in sunroom connects to the landscape. Facing: Screened by trellises covered in climbing roses and with brick underfoot, this breezeway constitutes a private garden getaway.*

*With a pool and poolside terrace perfectly*
*sited midway to the waterfront and with views in*
*all directions, the exterior living areas of*
*this property unfold in a composed landscape*
*that spans the cultivated and the wild.*

*Facing: Along our waterfront façade, the rooms open to a veranda with furnished living, dining, and gathering spaces. Columns mark the transitions from one area to the next. Rick's office occupies the room overhead. Above: The porch swing is a favorite spot for reading.*

*Via French doors, our living room extends out to this covered, curtained, furnished porch—a perfect place to watch the sun set in wicker seating that is easy to rearrange into different conversational groupings. Scatter stools double as convenient tables for drinks.*

*Above: An outdoor kitchen has an adjacent living/dining area for regular meals al fresco, one of the great pleasures of living in our southern coastal climate. Facing: For a guesthouse that often serves as a playhouse for the family's children and their friends, the covered porch has appropriate seating.*

*Facing: Wood garden furniture weathers over time and melds into the surroundings. The bold, bright glazes of the ceramic pot and the hot red blooms of the impatiens that it holds make a brilliant color statement amid the environment of grays and greens. Above: I love placing art in the landscape, especially whimsical pieces like this dog sculpture, which I purchased from the Bonner Gallery in Scottsdale, Arizona.*

# OUR LOWCOUNTRY BOIL

In the coastal areas of South Carolina and Georgia, nothing says summer quite like a Lowcountry boil. For those who have never experienced this wonderful pleasure, it is a classic one-pot feast. Just like the New England clambake, the Lowcountry boil celebrates the abundance of the season in a relaxed, delicious, happily messy way. There are no strict rules, nor is there a master recipe. Every good cook has his or her own favorite family variation, tried and made true over the years. That said, standard guidelines for this all-in-one meal do exist.

First and foremost, a Lowcountry boil emphasizes flavor and freshness. It starts with, and makes the most of, our wonderful local ingredients from both sea and land: shrimp, sausage, potatoes, and corn on the cob. Because it is a rite of summer and a meal that scales up easily to feed large numbers, it generally takes place out-of-doors: dockside, beachfront, poolside, and backyard work equally well. We're fortunate to have our own dock. We spend much of our summer out there because it is the one place where we can almost always catch a cooling breeze.

The Lowcountry boil, also known as Frogmore stew, has a storied history, though of comparatively recent vintage. Its roots extend farther back in time and place, however, to the Creole-style cuisine of the Gullah, the descendants of African slaves, who have long populated the Sea Islands and coastal regions of South Carolina, Georgia, and northeastern Florida. Lore credits the original recipe to Richard Gay, of Gay Fish Company, who hailed from Frogmore on St. Helena Island, deep in the heart of the Sea Island Gullah community.

Unlike its distant coastal cousins bouillabaisse and cioppino, a Lowcountry boil is not a stew, technically speaking. Conventionally, when the components are at just the right point of doneness, the host drains off the cooking liquid and transfers all the elements to a platter for serving. Another option is to spread everything from the pot out onto a table draped in newspaper, which keeps the cleanup simple. More often than not, we serve ours on a table layered with colorful linens, plates, and glassware, along with all sorts of condiments and sides. Then our guests and we gather to dig in and savor the very special pleasures of summer.

*We set up the table on our dock and then dig in to this classic one-pot meal that is a delicious melding of our regional bounty.*

*Above: Fresh lemonade is a favorite cooler on a hot summer day. Facing: We'll often linger on the dock long after sunset. Overleaf: The dock provides a perfect setting for our summer picnics, including our Lowcountry boil.*

# JONI'S LOWCOUNTRY BOIL

½ cup Shrimp and Crab Boil seasoning
(Zatarain's or Old Bay)

4 pounds medium red potatoes

2 ½ pounds smoked pork sausage links,
cut into 3-inch pieces

8 ears corn, cut in half

4 pounds medium shrimp, shell on, deveined

Fill a large stockpot with water, add seasoning, and boil. Add potatoes and cook 10 minutes. Add sausage and cook 10 more minutes. Add corn and cook 10 more minutes.

When potatoes are done (use a fork to test), add the shrimp. When the first shrimp floats to the top, they are done. Drain and serve.

# Afterword

My husband, Rick, our daughters, Sarah and Grace, and I feel that our lives are incredibly blessed. We see the many daily difficulties experienced by much of the world. Yet we are fortunate enough to be in a position where we can only imagine what it means to experience such troubles: to go hungry, to be homeless, to be without anyone to love or to love us. What we do know well is this: to those whom much is given, much is also asked. We also firmly believe that our children are our future. Over the years, these guiding principles have led us to participate in a number of community efforts on Hilton Head Island, from forming and building a Montessori School to creating a local bank to help support and sustain our region's smaller businesses. Our latest endeavor is the Valentine Project, a family mission to serve Tanzania's orphans and abandoned children. We feel privileged that so many others have joined us on this path.

Our goal for the Valentine Project is holistic and long-term: to shelter and provide complete care for each child the Valentine Project serves. To that end, the Valentine Project has spearheaded the construction of the Valentine Project Children's Home, an orphanage in Dar es Salaam. Designed and organized to meet the social, emotional, physical, spiritual, and intellectual needs of the children under its roof, this residence offers a safe, permanent, family-like environment for the children to grow through the years. A compassionate staff of five Tanzanians includes three caretakers called Mamas—the term the Tanzanians use for Mother—plus a teacher who comes daily to teach English, and a Mama's helper. Since it opened in July 2015, the Valentine Project Children's Home has become a loving home to nineteen orphans, ages three to seven.

From the Valentine Project's inception, there has been a strategic plan to allow for its considered expansion. The eventual goal is to build four more homes on the existing campus to shelter and raise as many as one hundred children. Partnerships with local churches and international service organizations are in place to ensure that the Valentine Project continues to maintain sustainability and accountability as it grows and evolves.

Like all such undertakings, the Valentine Project has been long in the making. It started as a twinkle in the eye of Bishop Valentine Mokiwa, a truly remarkable man. Rick first met the Bishop, who oversees the Diocese of Dar es Salaam, years ago on his first medical mission with our church to one of Tanzania's remote outposts. Since then, Rick has returned to Tanzania every year. In that time, Rick's relationship with the Bishop has grown, and through his auspices

*Rick and I believe that our children are our future, so as Sarah and Grace have grown, they have begun to participate more in our efforts at home and in Africa for the Valentine Project.*

Rick has developed a network of wonderful friends and colleagues in Tanzania.

Bishop Mokiwa has also frequently come to visit our community on Hilton Head Island. On his very first visit, Rick and I hosted a dinner to welcome him. That evening he looked at me and suggested that I come with Rick on his next trip to Tanzania. As Sarah and Grace were still very young then, to do so did not make sense for our family life. Several years later, though, the girls had grown up enough to go away to summer camp for two weeks. That was 2008. And Rick finally persuaded me to join him on his annual visit.

Rick and I had already started talking with the Bishop about possible long-term projects we might undertake. When we told the Rev. Greg Kronz, then the rector of our church, what we were considering, he decided to join us on our trip—and so did fourteen other friends. While we were in Tanzania that summer of 2008, the Bishop took us to visit a number of the archdiocese's ongoing efforts. He also explained his vision, laying out the various plans he wanted to accomplish in the coming years.

Like Rick, I fell in love with Tanzania on my first visit. I was particularly taken with the children, who are so beautiful—and especially with the orphans, so many of whom are homeless. When the Bishop took us to see an orphanage, Rick and I both fell in love with it as well. That experience was the beginning of the dream that has grown to become the Valentine Project. Naively, Rick and I just jumped in with open hearts. Only later did we begin to figure out how to proceed in a way that made sense.

Susan Ketchum, a friend who helped to form the Valentine Project with us, connected us with a group called Global Orphan, which began mentoring us through the development process. It was at that point that we realized we had much to learn about Tanzanian culture, and that if we didn't learn about the culture of the country and the ways of its society, we might do more harm than good to these precious children. With the help and guidance of Rev. Canon Dr. Alison Barfoot of Global Orphan, we set out to discover the best way to organize the orphanage we hoped to build one day. We visited orphanages and charities in Uganda, Rwanda, and Ghana, understanding more with each experience. We stayed on track.

With the opening of the Valentine Project Children's Home, we have now reached the next step in our long-term plan. Simon Musoke, the Director of Operations, handles the everyday administration. He is successfully bringing the Home to its next stage of self-sufficiency with a chicken farming operation to supply eggs for the children and also sell to the community. Sister Lucy, the Senior Mama of the three, is a firm, comforting presence and a steady force of good will, determination, and productive energy in the lives of everyone at the home and associated with it.

As Sarah and Grace have grown, they have joined Rick and me on our educational and fact-finding trips for the Valentine Project all over Africa. They have also been to Tanzania three times: when we started the project, when we broke ground for the home, and when we opened it. They love it and hope to take a gap year to live there between high school graduation and the start of college. I am sure they will continue to work with the

Valentine Project as they grow into their own futures.

Everyone involved with the Valentine Project has an eye to its self-sufficiency and sustainability in the years and generations ahead. A portion of the proceeds from our first line of textiles for Kravet, the J Banks Collection, aptly named Tanzania, will go to the project. Our local Rotary Clubs have joined with the Rotary Club in Dar es Salaam to build a deep, clean-filtered well to provide fresh, potable water to the home that the neighbors can also buy. There are goats for milk and a farm for growing cassava and other crops. There are cashew trees on-site and a grove of mango trees, with one tree for each child to tend.

Those involved with the Valentine Project and the Valentine Project Children's Home believe it is our responsibility to help care for the children of the world as they grow to adulthood. By focusing on the growing orphan crisis in Tanzania, we hope to have a substantial positive impact on the lives of the boys and girls now at the first Valentine Projects Children's Home, and on many more children as the Valentine Project grows in the years to come.

# Acknowledgments

would like first of all to thank our clients, who have so graciously allowed us to work with them and on their homes, resorts, hotels, and properties. Without you, there would not be a J Banks Design or a book. Thank you for your trust. This book would not have been possible without Jill Cohen. Her expertise and guiding hand were essential.

The same is true of Judith Nasatir, my writer, who found my voice and put together the many comments and conversations in a cohesive manner, and of the Ingalls, Gemma and Andy, who made our interiors come alive with much of the photography you see in this book.

My heartfelt gratitude goes to the talented art director Doug Turshen and his associate Steve Turner, who designed these pages to express our aesthetic down to the last detail.

To everyone at Gibbs Smith, and especially to my editor Madge Baird, I feel privileged to have had the opportunity to work with you.

All of you made this an absolute fun experience!

To the entire J Banks Design team, who shared their homes, clients, ideas, time, and support for this book, you have my gratitude—always. I could not do any of this without you.